DECREE IT

Using faith-fueled self-talk to increase your self-worth, confidence, and success

By:
Pamela D. Smith

Copyright © 2023 by Pamela D. Smith

All rights reserved, including the right to reproduce this book or portions thereof in any form whatsoever. For information, contact info@pameladsmith.net

Paperback Edition March 2023

For information about special discounts for bulk purchases, please contact info@pameladsmith.net

Pamela D. Smith can come to your live or virtual event to have a book talk or teach a workshop based on the content in this book. For more information, visit www.pameladsmith.net or send an email to info@pameladsmith.net

Scriptures are taken from the NIV version of the Bible. All rights reserved. Copyright © 2011 by Biblica

Printed in the United States of America

Library of Congress Control Number: 2023902910

ISBN: 978-1-7377896-7-3

To those who will decree that they are becoming more confident, increasing their self-worth, and experiencing a life of success.

Contents

Introduction 1
I am an heir to the Promise 9
I have the Mindset of Success 12
I Honor my source 17
I can discern the right counsel and coaching 22
Prayer is a part of my lifestyle 25
I plan for my success 28
I am Patient 32
I am Humble 37
I am in alignment with God's purpose for my life 40
I have integrity 45
I have Clarity 48
My Identity is in Christ 51
I am healed and whole 54
Reflection Time 56
Confidence Decrees 59
Confidence Decrees 60
Self-Worth Decrees 61
Self-Worth Decrees 62
Success Decrees 63
Success Decrees 64

Empowerment Word Search 65
Prayer for Confidence 68
Prayer for Self-Worth 69
Prayer for Success 70
Confidence, Self-Worth, and Success Board 71
Prayer Board 72
Scripture Board 73
Confidence, Self-worth, and Success Decrees 74
Author's Impartation 82

Introduction

If I ask you a serious question, would you give it some serious thought? I will go ahead and ask. In what areas of your life are you struggling to believe that you can possess what God promised? Why do you think you are struggling to believe in what has been promised to you? This is a question I had to ask myself. It took some deep reflecting. I had to go back several years to try to pinpoint what made me feel unworthy and what made me feel exempt from the promises of God. The reflecting stirred me up emotionally and it may do the same for you but rest assured that once you pinpoint it you will be able to heal and take authority over those defeating thoughts. You will be able to tell yourself something different about yourself. Something more empowering.

I reflected on my love for reading and writing. A reader, writer, and a church girl was how others described me when I was younger. Back then I did not know that writing was a way for me to use my voice and I certainly did not understand the power of my voice. Speaking never entered my mind back then. Strangely, I always had visions of myself in magazines. When I would share my visions with others, they would laugh, and it caused me to start second guessing myself.

I've always had a soft-spoken voice and it seemed as if no one took me serious about anything because I was so soft spoken. Somehow, I started to not even take myself seriously.

At 16 I became pregnant, and I gave birth at 17. I quickly went from being what others labeled the quiet girl to the girl no one wanted their daughter around. I was considered "fast" by some of the same elders who had once walked in my shoes. They showed no mercy or grace when we followed their example (sarcastic). I would hear stories about elders who were speaking over my life, saying that I wouldn't make anything out of myself because I became pregnant at a young age.

Shame, lack of confidence, and unworthiness creeped in. I did not recognize the internal damage that this was causing back then. I thought that since I made a mistake, I was supposed to be made to feel bad about it. In the eyes of the "church" I had committed what was unforgiveable by them. I had fornicated. I was even told that I would have to confess my sin in front of the church and ask the members to forgive me before I could start back fellowshipping at church. I complied because I wanted to be back at church, however I translated this experience to mean that I needed man's approval and that it was okay for man to condemn me when I made a mistake. I started feeling as if I was accountable to man. This made me feel so unworthy. It made me feel as if I did not qualify for the good things of God. I felt as if I needed to spend the rest of my life redeeming myself because Jesus' redemption for mankind no longer applied to me.

This church experience coupled with being teased for my soft-spoken voice, made me feel as if I did not have a voice. No one wanted to hear from me. I went on for years not honoring my voice, not understanding unconditional love, and not understanding forgiveness and grace. I was in church feeling this way. I was not nourished back into fellowship. I wasn't told that God still loved me and that He forgave me. But I was in church and being groomed by church people!!!!

I continued in school. I still graduated on time and on the honor roll, and I enrolled in college. I withdrew from college after my first year and a half and three and a half years after I had my first son, my second son was born. Yes, you guess it......I was really being frowned upon in my community and local church.

My husband and I married when our second son was 9 months old. We both had issues. We were young and both broken. I carried the baggage of not knowing what unconditional love, forgiveness, or grace was. I had experienced a combination of community and church hurt and internally I believed the story that they created of me.

My marriage was a hot mess the first few years. A real hot mess. Neither of us knew what we were doing. At this time, we didn't love, honor, or respect ourselves so it was difficult for us to affirm and cherish each other.

My back story is not one of not being taken care of as a child, experiencing homelessness, abuse, or poverty. Neither was it about a marriage where I was beat or cheated on, yet my struggle was still significant because when we struggle with our worth and knowing who we are in Christ then it's just as extreme as someone who is experiencing all of the aforenamed adversities. My struggle was internal while someone experiencing poverty, homelessness, or abuse has an external struggle. I struggled emotionally and it eventually manifested in the form of anxiety.

I experienced years of internal emotional struggle. It is what I called I.E.S. While going through I.E.S, I started having dreams. Dreams of being on stage with a microphone. I would wake up wondering what was that dream about because I was too soft spoken to have a microphone and too shy to be speaking on stage.

The dreams continued so I started sharing them as a way of looking for insight. Once again, I was laughed at. I was told that it was literally a dream because I was too soft spoken or too shy for any of those dreams to come to pass.

These dreams helped me to realize that my life needed structure. My husband and I attended the same college, but we had both withdrawn. I started feeling the urge to re-enroll. I then produced a plan. I would go back and obtain my degree and then we would relocate to a different city. I shared my plans with some people, and they did not believe I would move away. I went forward with my plan and re-enrolled back into college. Soon afterwards, our third son was born. Here came the judgement: "girl are you crazy having all of these babies?" I continued forward with my plan with three sons. I graduated college, but we did not move. At least not immediately.

I was working at the town hospital not knowing what God had in store for me and my family. I soon realized how God orders our steps to get us to where He wants us. We just must surrender to it. He tries to get us to not settle. Settling is a choice, but it's never God's intent. Things started changing at the hospital and I resigned and started working at a Home Health Agency. My plans for us to relocate were now two years behind schedule. Many around me told me that making $12 hour and having health insurance meant I had a decent job, and they could not understand me wanting more. I should have been comfortable they said.

For almost 2 years, things were going good at the Home Health Agency and then the environment changed. I helped a prayer partner of mine get hired there and one day while I was away at lunch she was fired. I was the Assistant Office Manager, and I was not included in the decision. It upset me terribly. I remember telling her that I was going to quit because I felt as if she had been treated unfairly. Her words to me were "I am okay. Don't you quit. You stand because there's some hidden things that are going on there and God is going to reveal it all and when He reveals it, it's going to lead you into your purpose." Less than 3 months later, our paychecks started bouncing. We would deposit our paychecks and get overdraft fees (well those of us who were living paycheck to paycheck like I was at the time. I didn't have money left over from the previous pay period to cover overdraft fees). Some payday Fridays we would get to work and be told that we would have to wait until the following Tuesday or Wednesday before we would receive our checks. The owners had started having financial issues. People started quitting. One of the staff members there started his own home health agency and a lot of the staff followed and went to work for him. It was not a good situation, especially for someone like me who was struggling emotionally and financially at the time.

I finally shared what was happening with a friend. She became upset and told me to quit. I remember telling her that I was not going to quit because God had not led me to do so. She thought I was crazy. She replied, "well you are not getting paid anyway. I would not be working and not getting paid or having my checks bounce." Every fiber of my natural being agreed with her, however I had started to grow spiritually, and my spirit wouldn't let me quit.

Remember I said in a few paragraphs back that I recognized that my life needed structure, right? Well during this time of financial turmoil on my job, I was adding some structure to my life and started to yearn a deeper relationship with God. My Mother and Godmother raised me to have structure and order. One day I heard God say, "I release you." I did not know what I was being released

to, but I understood that I was being released ***from*** disorder, financial struggle, and internal conflict. I knew that the release meant that it was time for me to leave my hometown as I had planned. Not long after, I moved to Houston, Texas.

The decent job, as described by those in my hometown, didn't work out long term but I believe that it was an ordered step by God. It was now time for Him to get me from what was familiar and comfortable so I could tap into my purpose. God wanted me to become confident in what He had put in me, to understand the power of my voice, and to understand unconditional love and grace. I moved first, got settled, and then my husband and children came later. Once settled in Houston, I started back writing. I submitted a poem, The Beauty of Color, that was selected in a poetry collaboration. I continued writing and then started self-publishing my books. Doors started opening for speaking and I later became a self-publishing consultant.

Throughout this journey, I have learned the power of our voices and the importance of what we tell ourselves. Sin separates us from God's love and causes us to believe the negative things that are spoken over us. It took me years to realize that my mistakes don't define me. This journey is also showing me that our purpose comes with different assignments and our assignments are seasonal. One season God may have us doing one assignment and then in another season He may have us on a different assignment, but it all aligns with our overall purpose.

I never considered myself as a Leader and I don't like using that word as a title. I believe that leadership is a behavior. It's a behavior that causes one to be able to make a difference, whether small or large, and help improve the lives or work production of someone else.

I wrote this book to help you understand the power of *your* voice and to help you see that you are the first person that you should be speaking life into. You can tell yourself the story that God has written **for** you and not the story that man has created **of** you.

I purposely wrote this book, so it reads as if you are speaking to yourself. This is going to train you to speak life into yourself and to speak greatness over yourself. As you read this book you will experience a newness. You will feel the spirit of God returning you back to that place of self-worth, self-love, honor, and respect. You will adopt the belief that because there is no failure in God, you will not fail. You will gain the courage to walk away from anything or anyone that dishonors, disvalues, disrespect, and doesn't love you.

Your life can change for the better if you have the courage to change your mind, tell yourself God's story plans for your life, and create new habits. You may have to confront some limiting beliefs because limited beliefs sabotages our ability to grow; causing us to forfeit a life of freedom and abundance.

It's time to Decree It and speak over yourself! Let's Grow.

Decree It:

I am breaking free from all of my fears, insecurities, and anything that has held me back from greatness

I am an heir to the Promise

"A relationship with God gives me access to greater."

Before you get deep into this, I want you to understand your position in God's kingdom. You are an heir to everything that God promised. You lack nothing. Job 22:28 says, "You will also decree a thing, and it shall be established for you; so light will shine on your ways." (NKJV).

A decree is an official order issued by a legal authority.

To decree is to state a fact.

Established means having been in existence a long time and therefore recognized and generally accepted.

This means that God has given you the legal authority to make an official order over your life, to state a fact about something that has been in existence a long time and is recognized and accepted. For the rest of this book, you will be stating facts about your life that God has had in existence for a long time and it's about to be recognized and accepted. Every word that you speak over yourself is a fact. It does not matter how your life has looked up to this point, if you want things to change you can start with decreeing. You have the legal authority to issue an official order to the enemy and let him know what the facts are about your life. Nothing he has thrown at you thus far has been able to take you down or keep you down. The power of life and life abundantly is about to be spoken over you and it's going to reverse every fiery dart that the enemy has tried to throw at you. The promise is yours. All you have to do is decree something different than what you have been exposed to, experienced, or encountered and a new thing shall spring forth for you.

Here are some self-decrees before you get started. Remember you are reading this book as if you are speaking over yourself. You are not reading this book as if I am talking about myself. It was strategically written so as you read, you are decreeing. I would even suggest reading it aloud. Make an announcement that you are about to possess what God promised you!

I decree that God is causing me to prosper.

I decree that all my needs are met according to God's riches in glory in Christ Jesus.

I decree that God has given me the power to get wealth.

I decree that God has mercy on me and He hears my prayers.

I decree that I seek ye first the Kingdom and His righteousness and all of these others things shall be added unto me.

I decree that from this day forward I am pressing toward the goal for the prize of the upward call of God in Christ Jesus.

I decree that my mind is always set on the Spirit, which is life and peace and not on the flesh which is death.

I decree that God's plans are to prosper me and give me hope and a future.

Decree It:

I value honesty, transparency, and credibility over perfection therefore I move when God says move.

I have the Mindset of Success

"The mind is critical to our progress and our direction in life."

Success first begins in my mind. The Bible places emphasis on the renewing of my mind. I understand that there are people and things that help shape my mind therefore my mind must be framed by God's truth and the principles contained in the scriptures. My mind is the seat of my intellect, and it guides my life. I am opening my mind so that I can make progress in life. I know that God desires to not only save my soul, but He desires for me to have a sanctified mind. I give God access to my mind, and I allow Him to frame it so that I only think pure and lovely thoughts. As I yield to the Holy Spirit, my mind will grow in a progressive fashion and conform to the ways of Jesus.

It is necessary for my mind to be set by the principles of God's word in my quest for success. My spirit, soul, and body was willed to God when I confessed Jesus Christ as my Lord and Savior. My will was broken, and my emotions were nurtured and tamed to do the will of God. My body has been employed and energized to carry out the will of God and what His intent is for my life.

Although my spirit was saved at salvation, my mind is still accustomed to the elements of this world and for this reason it must be renewed. My mind understands the language of the world because that is what it has interacted with since birth. I desire for the things of the spirit to be my language, my understanding, the core of my being. I understand that this new language must be learned while the old language be unlearned simultaneously.

By faith I confess that how I once understood is being replaced by a new, higher, and better understanding. What I once thought was success has now been refined. My perspective is changing. My view of the world is changing. A new day is dawning.

I understand that if my mind is not purged and refined by God, then I will not be able to understand spiritual truths. I understand that if I do not renew my mind then I will not be able to possess my promise. I remind myself of what Paul stressed in Romans 12:2,

"Do not conform yourselves to the standards of this world, but let God transform you inwardly by a complete change of your mind. Then you will be able to know the will of God-what is good and is pleasing to him and is perfect." Good News Translation

This scripture stresses the importance of me not conforming to the world. The world's definition and way of obtaining success should not be the way that I attain success. The alignment of my spirituality and success is vital if my goal is to not fail. I must adopt a higher, God standard-which I must allow God, through an inward transformation, to cause a complete change of my mind and this will cause a total overhaul of how I think so that I can fully grasp God's perfect will where my success (and all matters of my life) are concerned.

This inward transformation will bring a complete change of my mind when I "Let God."

Transformation lies in this command to "let God." This means that I allow, I give chance, I give room, I permit. I must permit God to do what only He can do. He can renew my mind to the degree that I allow Him to….and I am completely allowing Him to do it.

In letting God, I relinquish my will to Him. I completely surrender. I am ceasing to call my own shots. I am no longer sitting in the driver's seat. I give up my key. God is now in charge. He is charting my course. The Holy Spirit is dismantling every worldly, self-focused, God-denying philosophy and is stripping a mentality of failure from my mind. A glorious transformation is happening, and I am assured that I will not fail. This transformation is touching every part of my being. I am being changed. My mind is being completely changed. I will start to look at success from the perspective of the Spirit. Contrary to the principles by which I once operated, I will now begin to live out the will of God for my life.

I adopt a new belief system. One that is molded by God's word. I know that I assign things meaning based off my belief system so my new belief system will assign things of the Spirit significant meaning. I will also identify limiting beliefs, those things that do not serve me. I must ask myself, "why do I believe what I believe? Did someone speak a thing over me that caused me to believe this? Did I have an experience that left this impression in my mind?"

Truth is, I am a woman of God. My success in life is determined by my faith. It is defined from the being, character, and nature of God and not on my circumstances. The path has been laid out for me. God is the defining measure for my success, joy, peace, abundance, and a life well lived.

When I use the word of God to renew my mind, excellence is produced. Excellence then becomes a part of my identity. I start giving attention to details in everything I do. As my mind continues to be transformed, I understand that God is the one at work through me, I am just yielding to His plan.

Decree It: The Spirit of God is purging, pruning, and purifying me. I daily bow in the presence of God, and I invite the Holy Spirit to take full control. He lives within me. He moves throughout me. He takes over my mind and He tames my tongue. Being in His presence, strips me of fleshly wants and desires and brings me into alignment with what God has willed for me. I am a walking example of God's goodness and glory. I am a woman of faith and fortitude.

Decree It:

My pain was not a penalty, but a pathway to get me to my purpose.

I Honor my source

"I trust God for all of my needs."

God is teaching me how to be content as I model diligence and smart work in my quest to live a life of abundance. Honoring Him helps me to enter the reality of His promises to me. I envision a glorious life.

It is not enough for me to recite Psalm 23, but I must believe every single line and word of the Psalm. I trust God as my shepherd. He can lead me to green pastures. He has everything that I need. I am deepening my faith.

God knows the way and He can drive me to my destination. I get out of the driver's seat, and I hand over my car key of life to God and I allow Him to take the wheel. I move in trust because I know that God is committed to His word and His promises to me. His words are companions of His nature and character. Because His ultimate commitment is to Himself, it is impossible for Him to lie. Everything that He promised me shall come to pass because I trust Him as I apply the principles of His word to my life.

My trust and dependance on God leads to my personal discipline. My personal discipline is shown in how I power through fleshly impulses that do not honor God. It is shown in my self-restraint. It is seen in my commitment to nurture my spirit man. I develop a plan to live the God life and I commit myself wholly to executing this plan. I take action daily. I am not overtaken by the temptations of the world and the multitude of paths that are available to follow. God is my way.

When I see myself falling short, I confront myself with truth. I have a heart to heart with myself and I remind myself of the false image of self-worth that the world offers. I tell myself how important it is for me to break the chains of cliché's and to hold onto the freedom found in Christ.

I am a noble woman because I am a daughter of God. I do not run away from my responsibilities. I hold myself accountable and I resolve to remain committed. Bondage is not God's idea for His daughter. He gave me Jesus Christ as my Lord and Savior so that I can live and move in freedom.

I refrain from competition. How well I am doing in comparison to someone else is not how I measure whether I am successful or not. I desire for my light to shine so that others can be drawn to Jesus, but I do not desire the spotlight. I understand the difference. I do not yearn for the accolades of people. Unhealthy comparison will not be fueled by competing. I find fulfillment in what God has graced me to do. My motivation is not to outdo the next person, nor will it ever be. My continued personal growth supplies me on my quest for excellence and joy.

I am content but I do not settle. Being content does not imply resignation of God's will for me and the desires that He has placed in my heart. Being content means I accept my life where it is currently at, I live within my means, all while investing in my personal development to forge a new reality of God's promises. I don't accept self-defeat as it is not a quality of a noble woman. Contentment does not deny me the right to pursue better. I just make sure that I pursue better within the provision of God's word and will for me. As I exercise contentment, I do not arrive at my dreamland by any means necessary. Contentment is a moral quality and is necessary in my waiting period of God elevating me.

Being content does not snap the life out of my visions. It's okay for me to be content in my current state, while at the same time planning for and working towards more. I live within the resources available to me now. I do not try to cut corners or outsmart God's process. I am thankful for the gifts that He has given me. I enjoy the fruits of my labor and use it all for the glory of God. God's blessings for me are God-sized so it's okay for me to aspire for riches in Christ Jesus. It is okay for me to dream big. God enables me to get wealth. I aspire to create this wealth through my dependance on Him.

As I learn to accept and live within the available resources within my reach, I continue to develop skills and advance in my personal growth and development. I also improve my current skills. I have clear goals set before the throne of God and I pursue them wholeheartedly. I only compete with myself. My competition is with the woman I was yesterday. It is with the woman I was a few hours ago. This is how I continue to grow. This is my way of becoming better. This is my pathway to personal development, spiritual growth, and professional growth. This is my only way to compete, and this way makes my journey to self-worth, confidence, and success easier.

Decree It: God rules and reign in my life. There is no power greater than His. The mind that is in me is also in Christ Jesus. The power of the Holy Spirit helps me to triumph in life. My life is filled with unspeakable joy. I can stand boldly and take authority over everything that is meant to destroy me. God's strength is made perfect in my weakness. I denounce every wicked and evil word,

Decree It

thought, or deed that has been sent my way. I render it powerless. It has been returned to sender and sealed with peace and love. Love destroys evil work. Love brings destruction to the work of the enemy. Love changes the heart of those who meant if for my evil. Nothing can stop, hinder, overthrow, or block what God has for me. God is lifting me above it all. My mind is restored, and my strength is renewed. I am not enslaved to my thoughts. I have the power to change my mind from anything that does not bring peace. The lies of the enemy and the tricks of evildoers have been diminished, in the name of Jesus. My thoughts are ascending higher.

Decree It:

God is doing a new thing in me. A reinvention is taking place.

I can discern the right counsel and coaching

"The one who asks for directions does not get lost"

– Old Adage

My existence can be fostered through the right community. Community gives me a guided passage through life. God does not leave me without examples for the assignments that He has given me. I understand that if Jesus Christ was dependent on God, I must also be totally dependent on God. In order for me to continue in greatness, I must embrace those who have Godly wisdom and rely on their counsel. Sitting with the right counsel is vital. Impartations from the experienced is key. Who I seek counsel from plays a critical role in determining my outcome of the decisions I make.

Without proper counsel, my life becomes unstable. I meditate on 1 Kings 12:6-7 NIV, *"Then King Rehoboam consulted the elders who had served his father Solomon during his lifetime. 'How would you advise me to answer these people?' he asked. They replied, 'If today you will be a servant to these people and serve them and give them a favorable answer, they will always be your servants.'"*

I understand that elders have rich experiences that they can advise me rightly on. Servanthood is my ultimate assignment. As Christ Jesus was a servant, I must be also. Proper counsel and coaching will help me with solving problems, without violating my morals. My desire to grow will cause me to seek counsel that aligns with my spiritual and personal growth goals. God gives me strategies and ideas through the right counsel. He is an embodiment of wisdom, and that wisdom is transferred to me. God knows my beginning from my end. His unsearchable truths are shared with me. Through the intimate fellowship of prayer, I am invited to surrender my heart to Him. God has prominent place in my life. He has all of me. No part of my life is held back from Him. Through prayer, I receive revelation on who I should connect with. Understanding that I need counsel in my journey of growth, self-discovery, and abundance but more importantly is understanding that I need the right counsel.

Decree It: God's work in me is perfect. I am created in His image. I am perfect in His sight. I am who He says I am. Because I am coachable, I go from milk to meat. My life ministers to others. My transformation is never ending. I give attention to my personal development and my life continues to progress.

Decree It:

I am entering everlasting freedom, peace, and joy. My circumstances will no longer dictate my mood.

Prayer is a part of my lifestyle

"My peace and power is found in God's presence"

God is in time but not bound by time. When I pray, He comes through on time. Because His timing is perfect, I tell myself "Do not be anxious about anything, but in everything, by prayer and petition, with thanksgiving, present your requests to God."- Philippians 4:6 NIV. God invites me into His presence.

The things contained in the Lord's prayer are at the heart of God, so I focus on these things, and they give relevance and power to my prayers. Through prayer, I commune and fellowship with God. I do not allow my burdens and worries to replace God's ability. I denounce my emotions and do not give in to overwhelm. My actions do not put emphasis on my pain and problems because I believe that God cares for me and that He will help me. He is my very present help. My problems are not amplified. To do so is to diminish what I know about God's power. I make God's ability my focus and His majesty and glory becomes more evident while praying. His greatness is lifted high, and my problems are weakened. I yearn for more intimacy with God.

As I continue in prayer, everything else stands still in my life. God's presence and voice is all I concern myself with. His presence reassures me as I feel His comforting embrace. I do not want to let go. Jesus is being exalted. I ask for God's kingdom to take form in my life and take residence in my heart. I ask that it permeate every fabric of my existence. Thy kingdom come through me is my plea. When my world is fallen, may the kingdom of God reign in me. I listen as He leads and guides me. I eagerly wait for His leadership and direction.

When I am lacking what I need, intimate time with God reminds me that He gives me my daily bread. Everywhere I look in this world, there is a need, but I give thanks to God because He has not distanced Himself from the world that He strategically created. I surrender the pains and injustices and adversities of my family and my community to the cross of Christ.

God stretches out His arm with His unfeigned love to me and all of those in the world. My sins have not prevented Him from loving me. As He does not hold back His love from me, I won't hold back my love from others. The salvation of others is God's heartbeat so my heart must beat the same. I care about the welfare of others, and it becomes a honor to pray for others. I ask for the courage to forgive those who have trespassed against me, and I pray that His glorious will be done in their lives.

My prayers are to seek the establishment of God's will on earth. God's word has the capacity to deal with every issue known to mankind. I lay my life bare to Him. He knows anyway. I am intentional about asking that His will be done through me. My world is continued to be framed by His word. His word is fulfilling His intended purpose for me.

Decree It: My prayers connect me with God. He provides strength for my journey. I am being shaped and molded into a fearfully and wonderfully made woman whose light shines in dark places. I pray for others as I pray for myself. My lips are gracious and kind in my speech about others. Seasoned with grace, my prayers are a diving fragrance that moves the hand of God on behalf of those I pray for.

Decree It:

I don't have to be perfect to be purposeful

I plan for my success

"Always plan ahead. It wasn't raining when Noah built the ark"

– Richard Cushing

I must plan my work and then work my plan. How ever true is this popular saying. Planning helps me commit to the dreams and plans that God has placed in my heart. More than planning is my commitment to the plan. I will not allow a lack of commitment to stand between what I've planned and the fruition of that plan. Execution is necessary.

God committed, perfected, and fulfilled His plan when He sent Jesus to come to save me. And now I must commit, perfect, and fulfill His plans for me. No amount of prayers will get the job done if I do not take action. Praying does not offer me a shortcut from doing. Instead, prayer energizes me, it fills me with faith and hope, and it causes me to rise and do.

Intense commitment. Not halfheartedly. Even realistic plans will fail without execution. Planning and execution results in desired results. Anything less is just a model of a home that I can never live in. Beautiful and admirable, but unless I take possession of my dreams and goals, I can never live in the reality of them.

Proverbs 21:5 rings through my memory. "Good planning and hard work lead to prosperity, but hasty shortcuts lead to poverty." I will not surrender my life to chance or the wind. Neither will I surrender to the chaotic circumstances of the day. My focus is defined, and my aim is strategic.

A haphazard life does not attract wealth, abundance, confidence, or prosperity so I rise to the challenge, and I do not become a product of happenstance. I am successful because I prayed and planned to be successful. I constantly develop my character and maintain my discipline. I do not wish my way to the God life. The essence of my life will not be defeated. My living will be with purpose and meaning. I have drive and focus. I'm on a quest for excellence. Not perfection, but excellence. Nothing else will do.

I am productive in my daily efforts. I master my time. This is the key to my productivity. I define and determine what I will do each day. I put my goals on paper as this creates a sense of ownership and personal engagement to them. I don't postpone until tomorrow what I can achieve today. I'm like a farmer who expects a bountiful harvest. I do not refuse to plant my seeds.

I manage my resources well. My values are aligned, and I prioritize accordingly. I live meaningful. My time is not wasted on meaningless internet searches. I will not be lured into satan's den. I am disciplined in this area. The never-ending illusion of glamour that is on tv does not rob me of my time or purpose. The appeal of luxury does not drag me into idolatry.

My time with other people is well spent and not for the sake of gossip. I know how to put an end to conversations that veer in this direction. I take daily inventory of my life. I reward myself when it warrants it and I celebrate victories. I always reflect on my actions and remind myself that my life is a gift suspended in time, so I enjoy every moment. I am a great steward of my time.

Decree It

Decree It: Nothing in my life happened ***to*** me, it happened ***through*** me. I embrace the lessons in the things I experience. My mind and heart are open to the wisdom of these experiences. I can change the world by changing myself. I can change myself by changing my habits. I can change my habits by changing my decisions. I can change my decisions by changing my thinking. I confidently walk in my purpose. I am thankful for my gifts, talents, and calling. I will not get weary in well doing. I recognize that it is an honor and a privilege to be chosen by God. I trust Him to establish my plans. I am wise in my living. I will make the most of every opportunity. My life will reflect my heart and it will bear the fruit of the spirit.

Decree It:

I have the courage to face the giants of fear, doubt, and insecurity

I am Patient

"Waiting is not the last thing that I want to do when I'm not waiting in vain."

I am patient. Whether I am waiting for my coffee in the coffee shop, waiting for the traffic light to turn green, or waiting for God to bring a promise to pass in my life, I am patient. The advancement of technology does not cause me to be anxious. I do not allow a microwave mentality to redefine reality for me. I know that God is precise and on time. Patience becomes a virtue and a value in my evolving world.

When I have carefully crafted my plans and things still do not line up, I do not get in a panic. What is on my paper may not be in God's plan. I understand that life may present some undetected problems, but I will not waiver in my faith. I will contend with the uncertainties of life and make patience an important companion. My journey to the finish comes with a waiting period. This is the time where the quality of my character is shaped. This is the time where my attitude is refined, and a new woman emerges. I am patient because I am focused on receiving the promises of God.

My season of waiting may look as if the destination is not in view. I remind myself that my current location and my destination may not look alike. Even though my destination may appear so far away, I am joyfully patient.

As Moses was patient for 40 years, I will allow the wait to groom me for divine service. As Jesus was patient for thirty-three ½ years, I too will be joyfully patient. Today's get it quick schemes will not drown or devour me. I will not embark on a search for getting to the top faster than what God intends. I will not despise small beginnings. I am willing to start small and grow from there. I will not jump steps. I will not lose myself by being in a bid of quick success.

Patience helps grow my capacity and character for the destination that God is leading me to. I understand that my life will not outgrow my capacity neither will my career or business outgrow my skills. Patience helps me to be able to manage things well when they arrive. It is less difficult to tame a lion cub than it is to tame a grown lion and so it is with success, confidence, and self-worth. Success out of divine timing becomes sorrowful. Confidence wild becomes cockiness and misaligned self-worth becomes arrogance. Therefore, I am asking God to help me to attain leadership, people management, financial, communication, and self-evaluation skills. I desire for my personal value to increase before my financial value increases.

There is a time allotted for me. I can beat an iron into shape when it is red-hot, but it is difficult to beat metal into shape without heating it in the fire therefore, I will not be insensitive to God's timing for me. Waiting expands my faith and dependence on God. My dependence on God deepens my relationship with Him and thus the Holy Spirit guides me. Like the men of Issachar, I understand timing. Just like Jesus not going into the temple because His time had not yet come, I must wait until my time comes. I work while I wait. I feed my soul the Word of God and make my soul fat on the truth of it. I am active in Kingdom promoting activities, and not religious, church confined activities.

God does not seek to bless an idle life so my waiting is not translated into idleness or dormancy. I invest in my overall growth while waiting, not just on God, but while waiting in God. My waiting period is a time to polish the gift(s) that God has given me. Yes, the gift is free, but the polishing is sold separately. I want to represent the Kingdom well with the use of my gift(s). I am charged with being faithful over the gift that God has trusted me with. I don't dare pray for an enlarged territory if I am not stewarding well the gift that God has given me. God freely gave me my gift to serve as well as prosper from. I honor my gift. Because I have patience for when and how God will use me, He will divinely connect me with the people and resources that will help me go to the next level. I will make a bigger impact than I can imagine. My gift is needed by others so I want to take time to develop it so that I can effectively share my gift. Money is a reward of how I steward over my gift. My gift will not be used in vain or to impress others. God is the source of my gift and I look to Him for wisdom with the use of my gift. Patience serves me well and allows me to serve the marketplace well.

Decree It: I will patiently arrive at the place God has ordered for me. The beauty of the place is that it will be enjoyed with others who have allowed patience to take root in their lives. Patience is not an easy trait. Having it can be described as having a wilderness experience. Many days of discomfort and a lack of encouragement but despite that I will keep going. I must. To even think about what my life will be like if I don't exercise patience is devastating. From the day my journey began, I knew that my place of arrival was going to be a beautiful one. I have envisioned the tranquility of it. I have not been fooled into craving for perfection, but my soul has a space in the land of milk and honey that is reserved for me. The land where the grass is greener because the space that I once occupied was filled with doubt, and unworthiness, and negative self-talk. It was not that the grass needed watering there, that grass needed to dry out completely so that I could not return to such a barren land. I embrace this new space. A new mindset, a refreshed outlook, and a greater understanding of my purpose is resting here.

Decree It:

I don't fit the mold. I am a vessel of disruption. God is being glorified through me.

I am Humble

"Humility is not weakness, neither is it an indication of poor self-esteem."

What I know to be right and true will not be threatened by new philosophies. The word of God is the fabric that has held my world together. I live with the reality of being in a postmodern culture, but I cling to biblical truth. This new glamorous society leaves little room for humility. Pride stands tall, adorned with royal fabric. Although the world seems to be on a downward spiral; humbleness does not allow that to be the truth for my world. I take the position that God takes on humility. His position is uncompromising. The world's truth will not cause me to turn the truth of God's word on its head. While arrogance seems to be celebrated, God's word remains the same in Luke 14:11, "Everyone who exalts himself will be humbled, and he who humbles himself will be exalted."

I will not exalt myself for God will dethrone me. I will remain humble and allow God to take delight in exalting me. He will clear the way for my success. My success starts as a root and before it can blossom into a tree and be able to withstand the fury of the wind, there must be some spiritual and personal growth nourishment. My humility is my root that keeps me firm against the storms of life and allows my light to continue to shine bright.

I am a humble woman who accepts discipline and embrace opportunities to gain experience and grow. Wisdom becomes security for me and places me at a vantage point. God grants me grace because I am humble. James 4:6, "God opposes the proud but gives grace to the humble." God enables me to do excellent work. He commits Himself to my cause. I am a priority of God's. He opens His good treasure up to me. He does not withhold His love, strength, help, or Himself from me. Because I am humble, it can't be described what God is going to do through me.

Decree It: The glory of God is revealed through me. I always search within. I gave up the outdated version of me so that I can keep growing and elevating. I think different. I act different. I see things differently. I share my truth without fear of judgement. The other voices have been tuned out. Those voices can no longer keep me stuck. My decisions are no longer influenced by those who have no true understanding of my purpose. I am in tune with God and with myself, so I keep ascending higher. I am no longer enslaved to my past. I forgive in haste. I hold myself accountable. I partner with God to create happiness and I understand that happiness is a personal responsibility, so I snatch that responsibility out of the hands of others. I am no longer afraid to let people, jobs, projects, or relationships go if they do not align with my purpose. I accept the prerequisites to God's promises.

Decree It:

I am evolving beyond tradition. I am growing outside of the box of who others expect me to be

I am in alignment with God's purpose for my life

"Lazy people don't even cook the game they catch, but the diligent make use of everything they find."

– Proverbs 12:27 NLT

I can work like an ant and eat like and elephant when I am in alignment with my purpose. Being a diligent worker does not mean that I must work more. It does not mean that I have to endure more stress, consistently stay up late at night, or live a labor intensive life all the while having little to no money, little to no sleep, and little to no peace. This is what happens when I am not clear on my purpose and not in alignment with it. I connect the relationship between smart work and diligent work. I make use of my time and resources. Problems become goldmines when I know it is God's will for me to accomplish a certain thing. I believe in a better way.

I am not lazy or slothful. Working smart means I am selective in the things that I do. This means that it must all align. This helps to alleviate busy work, unnecessary stress and overwhelm. I work with willing hands, and I plan for the long term. I have been created as light and salt of the earth. I am not limited to the church as my destination, but the world is my destination so I arm myself with diligence and mental soundness in order to further the Kingdom of God. My purpose is not reduced to just work, but it contains joy and fulfillment. Purpose is not just a means to serve others, but through which I myself will also be served. Purpose gives my life meaning. Aligning with my purpose enables my creativity. Aligning with my purpose helps me to be fruitful and multiply. There is value in my purpose. My purpose is something greater and of higher value than money. My purpose is the innovative deployment of my calling in which through the fulfillment of it, I am worshipping God. Yes, being in alignment with my purpose is worship to God. It is also a means to finding personal fulfillment. I affirm Colossians 3:17 and declare that whatever I do, I do it to the glory of God. {"And whatever you do, whether in word or deed, do it all in the name of the Lord Jesus, giving thanks to God the Father through him"}. My purpose entrenches the primary reason for my existence.

Whether running my own business or working a job, I work for God and there is purpose in whatever God has willed for me to do. I remind myself that I am on a Kingdom assignment and that makes it easier for me to focus and excel in my assignments. I serve God with excellence using my skills and intellect. I offer the marketplace my best. I demonstrate the unconditional love in the marketplace. I am not blind to the suffering and brokenness of those around me. God uses me to minister peace and strength to them and he often use me to meet a physical need. This is purpose. I honor God by being excellent in the use of my gift. I am not a slave to money. Being a slave to money does not honor God. Being in alignment with my purpose allows room for self-care, self-maintenance, and quality time with my family and friend. I keep my physical health intact because my body is needed to live out my purpose. I am a vessel for Kingdom advancement. I employ diligence, excellence, and creativity in the marketplace, joining God as a co-creator of purpose.

Decree It: The promise keeper always delivers. I receive the desires of my heart. I will eat the good of the land. I will lend and not borrow. The fruit of my life will outlive any negative thing that has ever been spoken about or over me or any negative experience that I have ever had. God is catapulting me to my next level. Because I am committed to purpose, I separate myself from vain talk, filthy language, and wrongdoing. My time at my personal altar has increased. I repent as often as necessary, and I forgive quickly. I tap into miracles all the time. I emerge strengthened, redeemed, and enlightened. I choose to heal. I desire wholeness. I am willing to be purged and pruned, stripped, and chastened. My life is a sermon. It carries the gospel with it everywhere I go. I am salt. I season every space that I am in with love, grace, faith, and inspiration. I am resilient and purposeful. I am thriving. As I operate in my purpose, I am displaying power. I am unapologetic in the pursuit of my life goals. I do not allow my goals to be defined by how someone else sees me or what they feel as if I should be doing. God's will is the standard for me. I release what could have been and I do not allow myself to become scarred by what my plans for my life were. I put a guard around my heart so that resentment does not kick in like a soccer player on the soccer field. I know that resentment can come in strong and sturdy and the seed of it can harvest the fruit of bitterness, but not in my life. I denounce it now. I admit that the quality of my life reflects the choices I have made. My accountability yields strength, but it also requires ownership. I own my results in life. I picture myself in the fullness of who God created me to be. I feel the feel of it. I will no longer perform at a level that is beneath my potential. I will no longer enjoy the comfort zone. The change will mean growing pains. It means that I can no longer flow in the routine of ordinary. I must purge old habits, beliefs, actions, words, and even opinions. I must start filtering the information that I take in and only embrace and allow to penetrate, the things that are filled with joy, peace, and wisdom.

Decree It:

I eliminate the shackles of other people's opinions

I have integrity

"Integrity is not just in the way I do things, but it's who I am."

I have resolved to follow Jesus all the way. Integrity helps define my success. It implies wholeness, completeness, and unbrokenness. I will not tamper with or compromise the truth just to get ahead. I will not allow temptation to lead me from the essence and originality of who God created me to be. I will function as if God is always watching me, because He is. Having integrity means that my life is whole and unbending from the foundational values regardless of the prevailing expectations from the world. Integrity is my compass. It determines what I tilt towards when making decisions. It is woven into my character. There is coherence in my words and actions, in secret and in public. Every part of my life and every part of who I am is unified. Even in difficult situations, I remind myself that I am accountable to God and although a process may be difficult, if I remain in integrity, the end will hold great promises for me.

Decree It: I will not get caught up in an unrighteous culture. I will not allow what may be norm, but unpleasing to God, make me comfortable. Comfort can be a curse. I will not allow it to attach itself to me and control my progress, innovation, and vision. I will not allow it to point out the flaws of others who I have commonality with so that I make myself comfortable with what may be common. I speak over myself, and I break comfort's control. This is how I become empowered to change things, stand alone, and to go against the grain. I will not be influenced by the opinions of others. The Word of God will only influence me. I will not get caught up in what everyone else is doing or how they are doing it. I will only be caught up in the way the Holy Spirit instructs me to do things. The Holy Spirit gives me ideas, so I do not have to seek validation from others and lose my integrity. Transformation is possible for me. My past hurts, pains, mistakes, and misjudgments are the fuel that makes me continue to move forward and heal. I will not allow others to benefit from my brokenness therefore I will not remain in that state. I can make sound decisions. I set boundaries. I do not desire to stay comfortable. I will not miss the freedom that is found in Christ Jesus. My passion and purpose will fuel me on my journey as long as I remain in integrity. I change my perspective on the bad experiences that I have had. I consider those experiences as pruning. Pruning has helped build my character and endurance. Just as fruit trees must be pruned to bring forth the best fruit, I must also be pruned so that I can blossom into the divine being that God created me to be. I ask God to remove the dead leaves and branches from my life so that I am not going through life hanging and with a limp. I chant Matthew 7:20 NIV, "Thus, by their fruit you will recognize them." I will be recognized as a virtuous woman of integrity who is fully living in alignment with her purpose.

Decree It:

I don't have to pray for provision, if I am in purpose everything that I need is provided for me.

I have Clarity

"Clarity comes by delighting ourselves in the Lord and allowing Him to give us the desires of our hearts."

Every perspective that I have, every decision that I make, every situation that I face has been a result of what I believe. It is important for me to have clarity about who I am and what I should be doing with my life. Even when I know the **what**, I must be clear on the **how**. I will seek God about it all. This is where real clarity comes from. He may not give it to me all at once, but He will give it to me as I am ready for it. There is no clarity on my next step until I have fulfilled God's command of my last step. My desire is to serve the Kingdom the way God wants me to. He will give me understanding. He will guide my mind. His word will nurture my mind as I open it up to receive divine instructions from Him. I ask God to frame my mind. Although my mind is accustomed to the elements of this world, I surrender it to God right now in Jesus name. The language and instructions of this world are being replaced with Heavenly language and spiritual clarity. All that I do is in unity with God's will for me. My relationship with Jesus is the defining measure of my success. Clarity allows me to give attention to the details that God wants me focused on. The eyes of my heart are enlightened, and I know the hope of my calling.

Decree It: To see change in my outer world, I must change my inner world. I put an end to emotional suffering, inner criticism, and self-sabotage. I enter the fullness of joy. God called me to this space. Each day is a day for me to live purposefully, to demonstrate my faith, and to be a light in the world. I am telling a different life story. It ends well. My story is no longer from a place of pain and pity, but from a place of power and purpose. My narrative shifts to "look what the Lord has done." God uses me to minister to those who are like I once was. Ministry is not a word that terrifies me because I understand that ministry is not narrowed down to a pulpit or a podium. Ministry is my assignment to make others better. Ministry may not even involve me being in a church setting if God can be glorified and those I am serving can be edified. The enemy of my thoughts has been defeated. The enemy of misguided beliefs has been defeated. I believe what God says about me and I walk in the fullness of it. I will no longer allow myself to be robbed of the right to live a purposeful life. I heal from the things that have misaligned my thoughts and actions. Inner healing is strength. It is power. It is a demonstration of my faith. It is an answer to my prayer for abundance. No matter the weight of a burden that I carry, the depth of my brokenness, or the pain from a festering wound in my heart, God's plan for me is redeeming me even now! I am detaching from emotional turmoil. Emotional instability is not my norm. I am not what I went through. I no longer have an identity crisis. I am who God says I am. I am taking my power back. My voice is rising. I will start to experience a level of freedom that I did not know existed.

Decree It:

My presence is significant. God is awakening my voice to bring transformation to others.

My Identity is in Christ

"I am who God says I am"

Knowing who I am in Christ gives me access to authority, power, and influence. I see myself as God sees me. My true character and identity is in Him. No mater how I dress myself up, the core of who I am is spiritual. I am God's. God knows me. I cannot hide my true self from Him.

I am more than titles and labels. I am a nurturer. I am bold. I am courageous. I am fierce. I am filled with faith. There is nothing in life that I can not cultivate, grow, possess, own, or be because of who I am in Christ Jesus. My make up is integrity. I am clothed in kindness. My image is the part because my life yields the fruit of the Spirit. I allow the things that are on the inside of me to radiate on the outside. I am authentic and I do not look for outside approval. I am God's.

I am so secure in who I am in Christ Jesus that I am willing to change the things about myself that needs to be changed. I am willing to be healed. My job description does not define my identity. The things I do for my family does not define my identity. I have such a healthy image of myself that I am not phased by how high I may rank in a company, nor am I diminished by my lack of not having a Senior role. My identity is based on who God created me to be and is not based on what I may have been hired to do. I know myself. I have searched my soul, and I am allowing the light of my soul to shine through my being and reflect my Christ like identity.

Decree It

I am whole so I am not swayed my other's opinion of me, or their lack of knowing the real me. I am convinced that just because I may not live life in the exact same way as someone else, does not make my living in vain. I do not do things that violate the safety or well being of others, however I do not solicit opinions on how I should be living.

I keep first things first. I stick to my core values. I have faith in myself. I have laid a solid foundation for my life, and I continue to build on that foundation. I hold steadfast to my identity so that life does not sift me as wheat. I stand firm against the wiles of life. I am mastering the art of seeing things through.

Decree It: I am created in the image of God. How impressive is His creation. Fearfully and wonderfully made, I believe what His word says about me, and I show up in life accordingly. I do not think more highly of myself as I ought. I love me. I care for me. I honor me. I am a reflection of the goodness of God.

Decree It:

I spend more time focused on *my* purpose than I do watching others live theirs.

I am healed and whole

"Inner healing is a balm to the soul"

Without inner healing, my soul feels robbed. It feels as if a thief came in the middle of the night and removed all my family's personal belongings with us standing watching them. Without inner healing, I feel helpless, and I feel hopeless, thinking that there is nothing I can do but take it. I will no longer go through life holding on to pain, trauma, and emotional disturbance as if I have to just take it; telling myself that it's just life. I no longer buy into the cliché' of "what doesn't kill you makes you stronger" because pain and trauma kills self-esteem, it kills joy and peace, and it kills mental stability and one's zeal for life.

I break free from the cultural norm that shunned away from inner healing and therapy. "Just praying" about it is not a magic potion. This kind of teaching will no longer rob me of freedom and purposeful living. If I need therapy, I need therapy. I will continue to pray, but sometimes I will couple prayer with a practical technique. Therapy and a desire to be healed emotionally does not make me a weak Christian.

My emotional healing starts with me making a commitment of wanting better, wanting different, desiring freedom, and desiring peace. It starts with admitting that everything is not always A-okay. I admit that jumping and shouting will not sustain my healing and penetrate my soul. It is a gratification of the flesh. These things are a temporary fix. I also do not use faith and prayer as crutches. I understand that these things can also be crippling if I use them to avoid commitment, facing truth, and making different choices.

My life not always being intact is not an indication that my faith is not real. I cancel that false ideology. I cancel the false ideology that my faith is not real if I have emotional scars. The desire to be healed and whole is real and it's a testament that I do have faith. It takes faith to admit that things are not always good. It takes faith to admit that God has had to restore my soul time and time again. It takes faith to admit that I once was lost and had it not been for God, I would still be lost.

Decree It: Healing is strength. It is power. It is faith. It is an answered prayer. It is taking God at His word. It is exchanging my weakness for God's strength. It is how I renew my mind and reclaim my life. My desire is to live in freedom, peace, truth, love, and abundance. I am well on my way.

Reflection Time

Take some time to reflect on things that you believe keeps you in bondage, which have kept you from feeling confident, worthy, and successful.

Sit in silence and reflect until you can come up with 10 things. List them here.

I believe these things have kept me in bondage:

_____

_____

_____

_____

_____

_____

_____

_____

_____

_____

Pamela D. Smith

Decree It

Decree It: I no longer believe the things that do not line up with the word of God. I have a new mindset. I accept the truth of God's word.

Now take the things that you once believed and create a positive, empowering statement.

For example, I once believed that God was mad at me for my teen pregnancy, and I was no longer a recipient of His grace.

I will now turn that false belief into a positive, empowering statement and decree: God loves me unconditionally. My mistakes do not exclude me from His grace.

Select 5 of your false beliefs to create new decrees.

1. _____
2. _____
3. _____
4. _____
5. _____

Confidence Decrees

Decree It: Based on the word of God, I am confident. I stand boldly in my confidence, and I decree:

- I am strong and courageous, according to 1 Chronicles 28:20
- ·I do not fear because God is with me, according to Isaiah 41:10
- ·I can be strong in the Lord and in the power of His might, according to Ephesians 6:10
- ·I do not throw away my confidence, it will be richly rewarded, according to Hebrews 10:35
- ·I have faith in him and through him and I can approach God with freedom and confidence, according to Ephesians 3:12
- ·I can approach God's thrown of grace with confidence, so I may receive mercy and find grace to help me in my time of need, according to Hebrews 4:16
- ·I say with confidence, "The Lord is my helper; I will not be afraid. What can mere mortals do to me? according to Hebrews 13:6

Confidence Decrees

Decree It: Because of what God has said about me, I am confident that my life is changing for the better. Therefore, I decree: (create 7 decrees to increase your confidence. They do not have to be from the scripture, but must be empowering).

Self-Worth Decrees

Decree It: Based on the word of God, I am worthy. I stand boldly in my self-worth, and I decree:

- ·God has numbered the hairs on my head, I am more valuable than many sparrows, according to Luke 12:7
- ·I am fearfully and wonderfully made. God's works in my life are wonderful, I know this full well, according to Psalm 139:14
- ·I was bought with a price. I honor God with my body, according to 1 Corinthians 6:20
- ·My beauty is from my inner self, the unfading beauty of a gentle and quiet spirit. I am of great worth in God's sight, according to 1 Peter 3:3-4
- ·I am altogether beautiful, there is no flaw in me, according to Song of Solomon 4:7
- ·I am God's masterpiece, according to Ephesians 2:10
- ·I am more precious than rubies, nothing desirable can compare with me. Long life is in my right hand; in my left hand are riches and honor, according to Proverbs 3:15-18

Self-Worth Decrees

Decree It: Because of what God has said about me, I am worthy of the good things I desire. I am worthy of a great life. Therefore, I decree: (create 7 decrees to affirm my self-worth. They do not have to be from the scripture but must be empowering).

Success Decrees

Decree It: Based on the Word of God, I am successful. I enjoy my success and use it to bring glory to God.

- ·I can do all things through Christ who gives me strength, according to Philippians 4:13
- ·I commit my plans to the Lord and they succeed, according to Proverbs 16:3
- ·I walk in the ways of the Lord my God. I know what He requires. I keep His decrees and commands and I prosper in whatever I do and wherever I go, according to 1 Kings 2:3
- ·I am faithful over little so God is making me ruler over much, according to Luke 16:10-11
- ·I remember the Lord my God for He gives me the ability to produce wealth, according to Deuteronomy 8:18
- ·Because I do not just talk about what I am going to do, I actually do it, there is profit in all of my labor, according to Proverbs 14:23
- ·Because I trust in the Lord and my hope is in Him, I am blessed, according to Jeremiah 17:7

Success Decrees

Because of what God has said about me, I am successful, and my success draws others to Him and brings Him glory. Therefore, I decree: (create 7 decrees to affirm my success. They do not have to be from the scripture but must be empowering).

Empowerment Word Search

```
S A R E E P R I D E R A C S P
U N S C R O C R O I L E U B
C O S O T I C H T E C R D A
C A D N U T D H C H C T A H
E H R F D P O I S E D R O W
S A N I T A E K N I N W A I
S C H D N O R V P C B O L R
R H T E A A H D E F A G H T
S E L F W O R T H F G G H T
A R T T V P R C B O L E L H
```

·poised ·pride ·honor ·self-worth ·confident ·gain ·success

How do I increase my confidence and self-worth so that I experience success?

Know what God says about me
Believe what God says about me
Decree what God says about me

This starts with me defining success for myself and not adapting to what the world says success is. Success for me may be to lose fifteen pounds in 4 months. Success for me may be to make an extra $10,000 every year. Success for me may be having a healthy relationship with my mom or my child. Success for me may be to get off the medication that my doctor has me on. It is different for everyone and it's personal. For me to experience it, I must be confident in what God is able to do through me and I must know that I am worthy of it. Success will not attach itself to the person who does not believe that it is possible and that they should experience it.

I increase my confidence and self-worth so that I can experience success by first knowing what God says about me. I search the scripture. I meditate on the scripture. I learn the scripture and I apply the scripture.

Secondly, I must believe what God says about me. I can search, meditate on, learn, and try to apply the scripture all that I want, but unless I believe what God says about me, it will not penetrate my heart and become real for me.

Finally, I must decree what God says about me. The proof that I know and believe what God says about me is evident in my language, in what I say about myself, in the way that I talk to myself and talk about myself. I decree what God says about me and this is how I increase my confidence and self-worth and experience success.

Prayer for Confidence

Heavenly Father, I come to your throne of grace with full confidence that you hear me and that you love me. I thank you for creating me in your image and likeness. I ask that you give me a renewed spirit of confidence. When I feel as if I don't have what it takes to accomplish something, may I be reminded that I can do all things through Christ who gives me strength. When I get caught up in comparison and feeling as if I can not do what someone else can do may I be reminded that I am fearfully and wonderfully made. You made me unique. You created me to stand out. I'm supposed to feel different because there is no one else like me. I challenge myself to daily put my heart in your hand. If I am feeling a lack of confidence because of internal issues, I lay those issues at your feet right now. God expose the secret things in my heart and show me myself. May your unconditional love cast down any self-destructive spirit that may try to rise up against who you have said that I am. I walk in pride and dignity, knowing that I am a daughter of the King. I hold my head up and I am confident in your plans for me. I yield to the Holy Spirit that gives peace to my mind, rest to my soul, order to my life, and strength for my journey. I am confident in you and confident in my ability to do what you have called me to do. In Jesus name. Amen.

Prayer for Self-Worth

Heavenly Father, I come to your throne of grace where there is grace and mercy to help me in my time of need. Lord, I know that you created me as a vessel worthy of honor. I commit to honoring myself before I can expect others to honor me. I ask for forgiveness for not fully honoring myself up to this point. I confess that any mess in my life could be a result of a bad choice that I made, and this bad choice could have dishonored me. I thank you for your forgiveness, Lord. I thank you for putting in me everything that I need to fulfill your purpose for me. I cancel the spirit of confusion. I denounce the spirit of dishonor. I take authority over self-criticism. God, I break free from the strongholds of habits and routines that do not honor my mind, my body, my life, or you. I rise up against it, in the name of Jesus. I take up my cross and I follow you because you have chose me, you have qualified me, and you have equipped me. I am worthy of doing what you have called me to do. I do not have to cut corners or take short cuts because I am well capable of accomplishing what seems to be impossible. You called me blessed so I am blessed. You called me favored therefore I am favored. You have called me worthy, therefore I am worthy. In Jesus name. Amen.

Prayer for Success

Heavenly **Father,** I come to your throne of grace thanking you for your good plan for me, the plan to prosper me and not harm me, your plan to give me an expected end. Success is my expected end. Following my God ordained path will lead me to abundance and prosperity. I thank you for clearing my runway Lord and giving me what I need to take off. I thank you that because you are within me, I will not fail. Shield me from anything that will deter me from accomplishing what you have planned for me. Guard my mind against anything that will cause me to develop an appetite for things that are not of you. I come against all distractions in the name of Jesus. I take on courage so that I can fearlessly take on the giants of distractions. I do not follow or lust over things that are not for me. I ask that you continue to order my steps in your word and let not any iniquity have dominion over me. I am assured that with you on my side, I will win. With you on my side, I will triumph. With you on my side, I will become all that you created me to become, and I will have all that you have willed for me to have. Success is my portion. My success will bring glory to you and will draw others to the Kingdom. I praise you for it. In Jesus name. Amen.

Confidence, Self-Worth, and Success Board

This is an exercise that you can do in this book, or you can get you a poster board (or any type of board) and cut out pictures. For this book, you can write words that make you feel confident, worthy, and successful.

Prayer Board

This is an exercise that you can do in this book, or you can get you a poster board (or any type of board) and cut out pictures of what you are praying for. (Example: if you are praying for peace, you can find the word peace and put it on your board or you can find something that resembles peace and use that picture. If you complete this exercise in this book, you can write the words in the squares.

Scripture Board

This is an exercise that you can do in this book, or you can get you a poster board (or any type of board) and paste scriptures that relate to confidence, self-worth, and success. If you complete this exercise in this book, you can write the scriptures in the squares.

Confidence, Self-worth, and Success Decrees

Decree It:

- I decree that the Spirit of God is activated within me, so I do not need to search externally.
- I decree that I will love my life and live my life according to God's plan so that when I leave my life it will be well with me.
- I decree that God walks with me therefore I will not stop just because I face a hardship.
- I decree that I am encouraged because I know that there is opportunity in opposition.
- I decree that I am equipped to manage each day with grace.
- I decree that I am empowered to live the abundant life that Jesus Christ died for me to live.
- I decree that I will remain hopeful in the face of adversity because the greater one lives within me.
- I decree that with God, I can conquer anything.
- I decree that I am not held captive to my past or stagnated by what could be in the future. I live in the now and believe that God will take care of tomorrow.
- I decree that I am empowered to make better choices.

- I decree that I own my flaws and I make great effort to change.
- I decree that I accept constructive feedback with love.
- I decree that I am passionate about growth so I am selective in who I allow to coach or mentor me.
- I decree that my purpose is not tied up in the opinions of others.
- I decree that I understand my value.
- I decree that I will no longer perform below my true potential.
- I decree that I will filter information. My spirit will only accept what is for me and what will help me grow. I will not allow put downs to infiltrate my spirit and make me feel unloved or unworthy.
- I decree that I willingly and humbly pick up God's plan, will, and desires for my life. I release my own and allow the Holy Spirit to guide me into what's best for me.
- I decree that everything that I do will be purposeful and meaningful. No more wasted time, energy, or focus.
- I decree that I believe in myself and will only do things that will make me a better me.
- I decree that I am not easily influenced by the opinions of others.
- I decree that I am not caught up in what everyone else is doing or how they are doing it. I am happy with me.
- I decree that I use my God-given creativity without seeking approval from others.

- I decree that I will make beneficial use of valuable information and resources.
- I decree that I will surround myself with people who are empowering and uplifting.
- I decree that I will love myself enough to make the necessary changes to improve my life.
- I decree that I will not seek perfection, but rather excellence.
- I decree that I must become a better me before I can empower and equip others to become a better them.
- I decree that I will honor my life, my purpose, my time, and my attention by doing what God has called me to do.
- I decree that I will not allow the past to hinder me from moving forward.
- I decree that my past is only a point of reference and not a place of residence.
- I decree that I will not allow anyone to talk me out of living my dreams just because they are not living theirs.
- I decree that I do not need validation from others.
- I decree that I will not allow anyone to make me feel guilty because I am pursuing my purpose.
- I decree that I will continue growing, succeeding, and learning.
- I decree that I will set goals and take actions that will thrust me into better.
- I decree that I will not trust in my own ability, but will trust in what God is able to do through me.

- I decree that I will not limit myself.
- I decree that I am a creative, spiritual being. My words shape my world.
- I decree that on the tip of my tongue is either my future or my funeral, so I speak life and a great future over myself.
- I decree that God gave me my purpose and has given me permission, so I now give myself permission, to pursue my purpose and prosper from it.
- I decree that I am strong and courageous. My thoughts are aligned with God's perfect will. I will push against fear and doubt.
- I decree that I am chosen for this.
- I decree that I am a witness for Christ. My purpose will bring glory to Him. I bring my thoughts, ideas, and plans into alignment with His will.
- I decree that as my mind is transforming, my thoughts are shifting from where I am to where I am purposed to be.
- I decree that my self-worth is not defined by my job description, physical assets, or money.
- I decree that I see myself as God sees me, nothing more and nothing less. I have a positive self-image and I am altogether wonderful.
- I decree that God created me in His image and His creation is awesome.
- I decree that kindness is my virtue. I freely give it.
- I decree that God's unlimited supply of grace is available to me.

- I decree that I operate from a graceful place, I am an illuminating spirit; a beacon of light.
- I decree that my conversations are always seasoned with positivity and pleasantness.
- I decree that I use my words to edify others.
- I decree that I listen intentionally so that I am able to accurately interpret what is being said with accuracy. I do not pre-judge or assume what someone is saying.
- I decree that I only exercise my freedom of speech around those who value my voice.
- I decree that grace shows up in my walk. I move about with ease. I step high and own each move that I make because God orders my steps.
- I walk with confidence, not arrogance. Every move I make is made consciously and with great intent.
- I decree that I am walking away from the person I was yesterday and stepping into the person God has made me to be.
- I decree that grace is a spark that sheds light on my buried soul and resurrects my spirit.
- I decree that my mind is expanding, my conscious is awakened, and my spirit is enlightened.
- I decree that I am growing into the person whom I have been in search of for years.
- I decree that I am not hard hearted.
- I decree that I will not use prayer as an excuse to gossip.

- I decree that I will use my tongue to edify others. I will speak well of others and use my tongue to encourage.
- I decree that the love of God is shed abroad in my heart.
- I decree that healing and restoration is a priority for me.
- I decree that the cycle of bondage has been broken in my life.
- I decree that I am mentally strong, spiritually strong, physically strong, and financially strong.
- I decree that all curses, evil words, words contrary to what God says about me, my children, or my family have been destroyed in the mighty name of Jesus.
- I decree that anything sent to hinder or disrupt my peace or life has been cancelled and rendered powerless, in Jesus name.
- I decree that my entire family is saved, delivered, and set free from the enemy's bondage.
- I decree that I am emotionally healed.
- I decree that I am confident, I know my worth, and I am successful.
- I decree that my loved ones will uncover their purpose and begin to operate in it.
- I decree that God is causing me to prosper and giving me strategies of which I have not thought.
- I decree that goodness and mercy shall follow me all the days of my life.
- I decree that I operate from a pure heart, with honesty, integrity, and love.

- I decree that I always walk upright.
- I decree that no good thing will God withhold from me because I walk upright.
- I decree that God uses me to help others transform, breakthrough, heal, and live abundant purpose centered lives.
- I decree that I am an example of God's goodness and favor.
- I decree that I am a Kingdom influencer, everything that I do is for the glory of God.
- I decree that my family is safe, protected, purposeful, mentally and emotionally healthy, and living a peaceful and prosperous life.
- I decree that me and my family are healed, whole, unified, and living in the promises of God.
- I decree that I live a life of simplicity and ease.
- I decree that the blessing of the Lord makes me rich and adds no sorrow with it. (Proverbs 10:22).
- I decree that if God does not order the step, I will not move my feet.
- I decree that I can be more by doing less.
- I decree that I will live the scriptures and not just quote them.
- I decree that I trust in the Lord with all my heart, and I do not lean to my own understanding. (Proverbs 3:5)
- I decree that I work from a place of rest and not a place of overwhelm.

- I decree that God opens the heavens and sends rain on my land and He blesses the work of my hands. (Deuteronomy 28:12).

- I decree that God is me and my family's rock in whom we take refuge, He's our shield and the horn of our salvation. He is our stronghold, our refuge and our Savior-from violent men He saves us. We call to the Lord who is worthy of praise, and we are saved from our enemies. (2 Samuel 22:3-4).

- I decree that me and my family are saved and walking in our purpose. God divinely protects us. Every arrow or fiery dart shot at us does not penetrate, but is shot down and destroyed by the blood of Jesus.

- I decree that me and my family are disciplined with our health and our wealth. Our minds are at ease and our lives are at peace.

Author's Impartation

Now that you have read this book and have decreed many remarkable things over your life, you may experience some opposition. The enemy may come to try to test the words that you have spoken. Do not give up or give in. The words that you have decreed over yourself are powerful and true. God is causing them to manifest, and you will see the fruit of what you know, believe, and decree.

I stand in agreement with you that your confidence is going to a new level, your self-worth is increasing, and you are about to experience wholistic success. As you move and live in this, I want to encourage you not to avoid tough conversations. Avoiding them will eat you up on the inside. The peace around you can not compare to the peace within you.

I also want to encourage you to execute on every goal that you set for yourself. If there is no execution or action plan, then you are merely dreaming.

Remember that inner healing is continuous, and you must be intentional about it. It is spiritual liberation.

Be determined to live a purposeful life and not a popular life.

The scriptures that you quote must be lived. If you have faith, then you will not keep making the same resolutions, reciting the same decrees and affirmations without acting. Your miracle and transformation is in your movement. At some point you will have to close the bible, come out of the prayer closet, and bust a move. This does not mean that you must live the way you see others living, or do what you see others doing, but you must be taking some action to move your life forward. Your wealth and abundance lies in the instructions that God gives you. Follow His instructions and you will create your wealth. The scripture, Deuteronomy 8:18 says He gives us power (the anointing, the creativity, the witty ideas, the resources) to get (create) wealth. It does not say that He gives us the wealth. Stop waiting on something to fall from the sky. Go and get what God has already said is yours!!

My Prayer for You

Heavenly Father, I lift up the person who read this book. I ask that your Holy Spirit will penetrate the pages of this book and bring transformation in their life. God, exalt them, in the name of Jesus. Fill them with confidence, self-worth, and success. Remove any sorrow, pain, agony, or grief that can sometimes be associated with success. May they follow the good plans that you have for their life. God as you bless them, I pray that they will be a blessing to others. I pray that from this day forward they vow to live a life where you can be glorified; a life where the unsaved will surrender to the cross of Jesus Christ; a life that is so filled with your glory that others will know that truly they are a son or daughter of God! In Jesus mighty name I pray. Amen

Thank You!

A big thank you for your purchase of this book. May God's best always be your portion.

Grace and Peace,
Pamela D. Smith

To book Pamela to do a Faith-Fueled Confidence, Self-Worth & Success Book Talk, go to www.pameladsmith.net

To request that Pamela lead prayer in your service or at your physical or virtual event, go to www.pameladsmith.net

I would greatly appreciate you taking time to submit a review here: https://g.page/r/CboBVAaQKzXREAE/review

Or send your feedback to info@pameladsmith.net

www.ingramcontent.com/pod-product-compliance
Lightning Source LLC
Chambersburg PA
CBHW070315120526
44590CB00017B/2695